EPISODE I
THE PHANTOM MENACE

STAR WARS®
EPISODE I
THE PHANTOM MENACE

Adapted from
the original story by
GEORGE LUCAS

Script
HENRY GILROY

Pencils
RODOLFO DAMAGGIO

Inks
AL WILLIAMSON

Colors
DAVE NESTELLE

Color Separation
HAROLD MACKINNON

Lettering
STEVE DUTRO

Cover Art
RAVENWOOD

STAR WARS
EPISODE I
THE PHANTOM MENACE
3D

DARK HORSE BOOKS®

Collection designer
KAT LARSON

Original series editor
DAVE LAND

Collection assistant editor
FREDDYE LINS

Collection editor
RANDY STRADLEY

President and publisher
MIKE RICHARDSON

Special thanks to Joanne Chan Taylor, Leland Chee, Troy Alders, Carol Roeder,
Jann Moorhead, and David Anderman at Lucas Licensing.

This volume collects *Star Wars*: Episode I—*The Phantom Menace* #1–#4,
originally published by Dark Horse Comics.

STAR WARS: EPISODE I—THE PHANTOM MENACE

MIKE RICHARDSON president and publisher **NEIL HANKERSON** executive vice
president **TOM WEDDLE** chief financial officer **RANDY STRADLEY** vice president of
publishing **MICHAEL MARTENS** vice president of book trade sales **ANITA NELSON**
vice president of business affairs **MICHA HERSHMAN** vice president of marketing **DAVID
SCROGGY** vice president of product development **DALE LAFOUNTAIN** vice president
of information technology **DARLENE VOGEL** senior director of print, design, and
production **KEN LIZZI** general counsel **DAVEY ESTRADA** editorial director **SCOTT ALLIE**
senior managing editor **CHRIS WARNER** senior books editor **DIANA SCHUTZ** executive
editor **CARY GRAZZINI** director of print and development **LIA RIBACCHI** art director
CARA NIECE director of scheduling

Published by Dark Horse Books
A division of Dark Horse Comics, Inc.
10956 SE Main Street
Milwaukie, OR 97222

DarkHorse.com
StarWars.com

To find a comics shop in your area, call the Comic Shop
Locator Service toll-free at 1-888-266-4226.

First paperback edition: May 1999
Second paperback edition: January 2012
ISBN 978-1-59582-841-5

1 3 5 7 9 10 8 6 4 2
1010 Printing International, Ltd., Guangdong Province, China.

THE RISE OF THE EMPIRE
1000–0 YEARS BEFORE *STAR WARS: A NEW HOPE*

The events in this story take place approximately
thirty-two years before the Battle of Yavin.

After the seeming final defeat of the Sith, the Republic
enters a state of complacency. In the waning years of
the Republic, the Senate is rife with corruption, and
the ambitious Senator Palpatine has himself elected
Supreme Chancellor.

Turmoil has engulfed the Galactic Republic. The taxation of trade routes to outlying star systems is in dispute.

Hoping to resolve the matter with a blockade of deadly battleships, the greedy Trade Federation has stopped all shipping to the small planet of Naboo.

While the Congress of the Republic endlessly debates the alarming chain of events, the Supreme Chancellor has secretly dispatched two Jedi Knights, the guardians of peace and justice in the galaxy, to settle the conflict. . . .

EPISODE I—THE PHANTOM MENACE

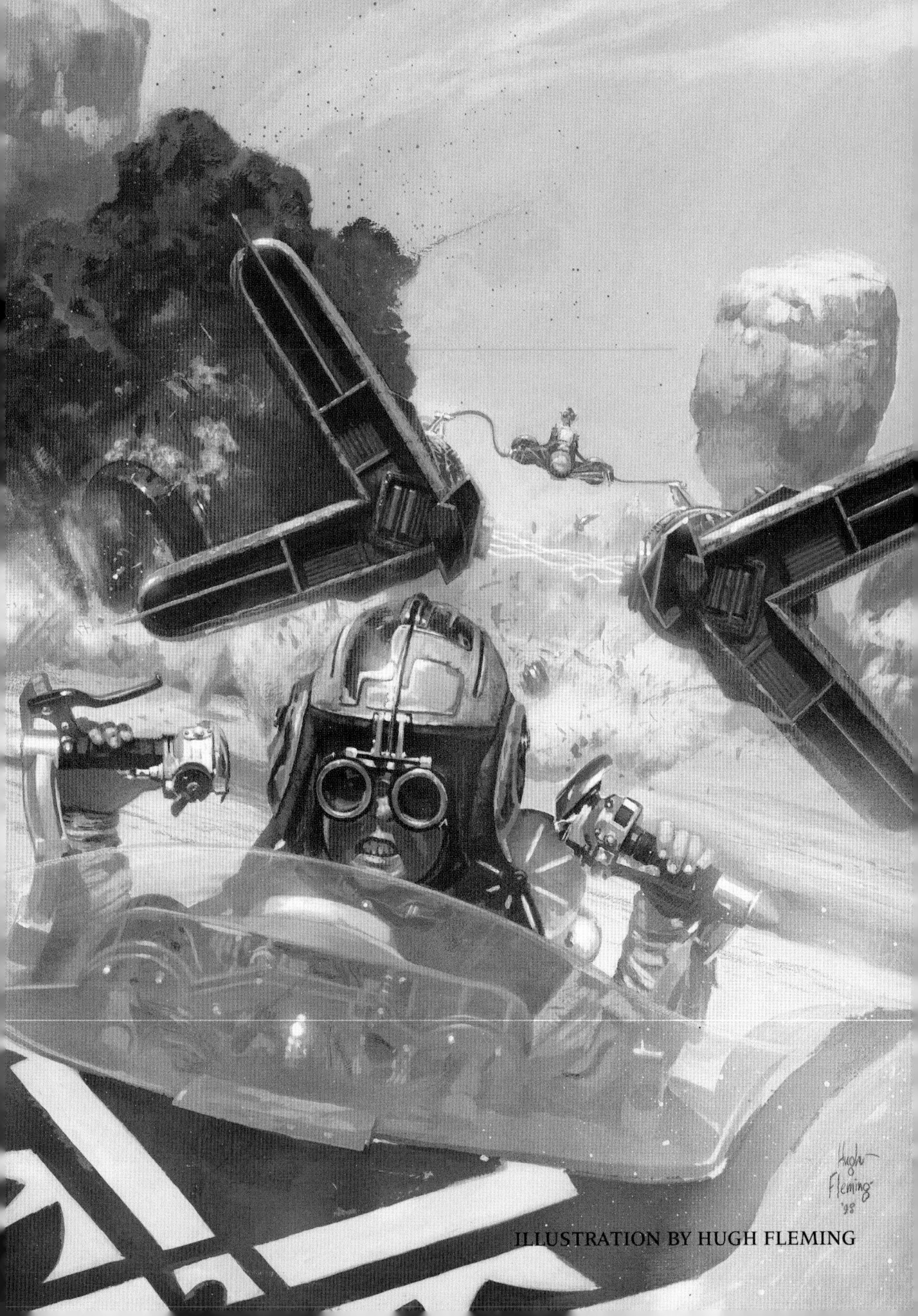
Hugh Fleming '98

ILLUSTRATION BY HUGH FLEMING

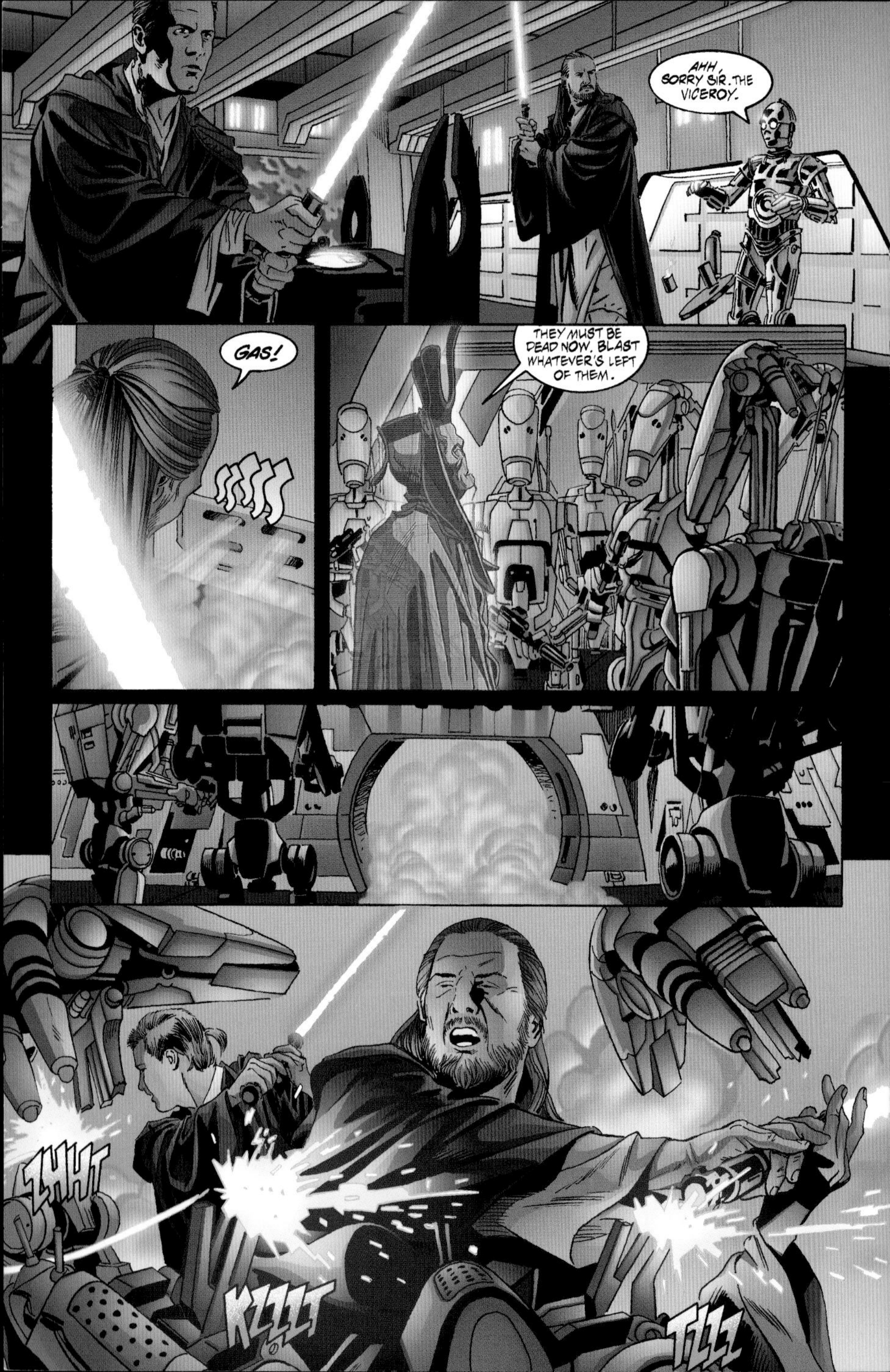
AHH, SORRY SIR. THE VICEROY.
GAS!
THEY MUST BE DEAD NOW. BLAST WHATEVER'S LEFT OF THEM.
ZHHT
KZZZT
TZZZ

AN EXTREMELY WELL-PUT-TOGETHER LITTLE DROID.

WITHOUT A DOUBT, IT SAVED THE SHIP AS WELL AS OUR LIVES.

IT IS TO BE COMMENDED. WHAT IS ITS NUMBER?

R2-D2, YOUR HIGHNESS.

THANK YOU, ARTOO-DETOO. YOU HAVE PROVEN TO BE VERY LOYAL.

WHOOT EEEET OOOO!

PADMÉ! CLEAN THIS DROID UP THE BEST YOU CAN. IT DESERVES OUR GRATITUDE.

YOUR HIGHNESS, WE ARE HEADING FOR A REMOTE PLANET CALLED TATOOINE.

YOUR HIGHNESS, TATOOINE IS VERY DANGEROUS. I DO NOT AGREE WITH THE JEDI ON THIS.

YOU MUST TRUST MY JUDGEMENT, YOUR HIGHNESS.

ON THE JEDI'S RECOMMENDATION, THE QUEEN ORDERS HER SHIP TO SET COURSE FOR THE PLANET OF TATOOINE.

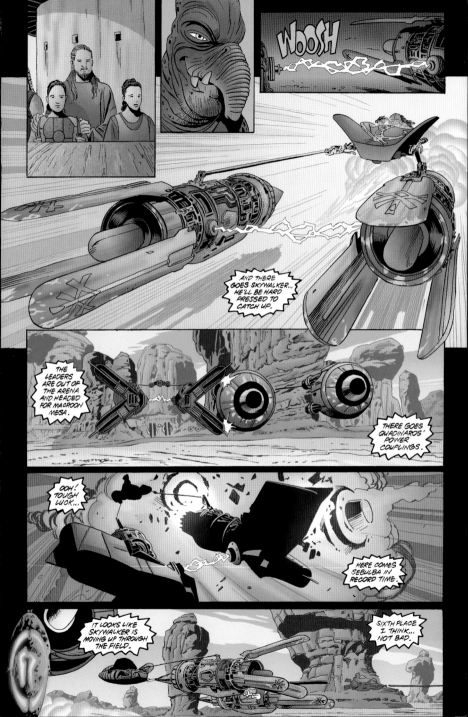

WOOSH

AND THERE GOES SKYWALKER... HE'LL BE HARD PRESSED TO CATCH UP.

THE LEADERS ARE OUT OF THE ARENA AND HEADED FOR MACROON MESA.

THERE GOES QUADINAROS' POWER COUPLINGS.

OOH! TOUGH LUCK...

HERE COMES SEBULBA IN RECORD TIME.

IT LOOKS LIKE SKYWALKER IS MOVING UP THROUGH THE FIELD.

SIXTH PLACE I THINK... NOT BAD.

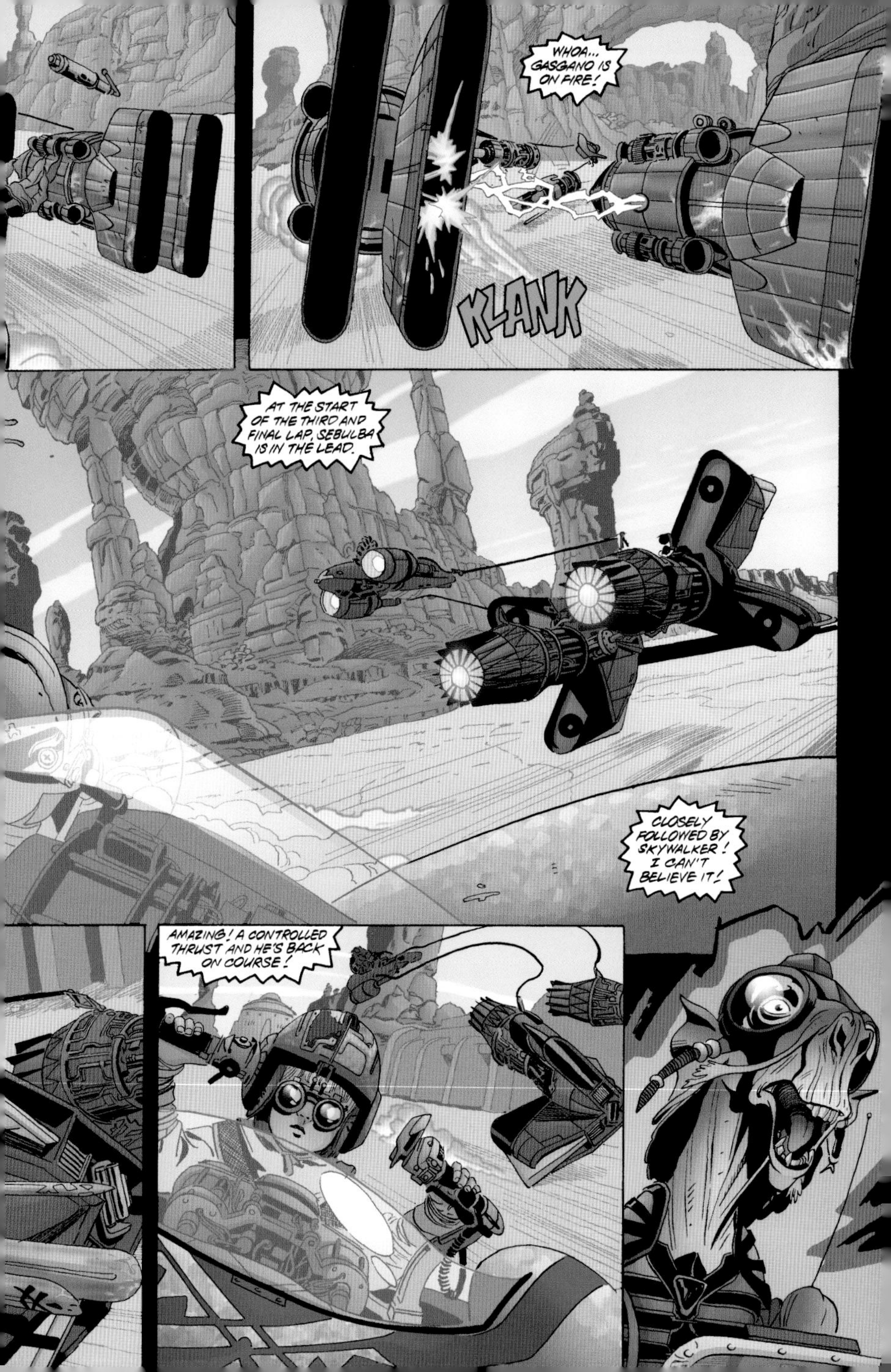
WHOA... GASGANO IS ON FIRE!
KLANK
AT THE START OF THE THIRD AND FINAL LAP, SEBULBA IS IN THE LEAD.
CLOSELY FOLLOWED BY SKYWALKER! I CAN'T BELIEVE IT!
AMAZING! A CONTROLLED THRUST AND HE'S BACK ON COURSE!

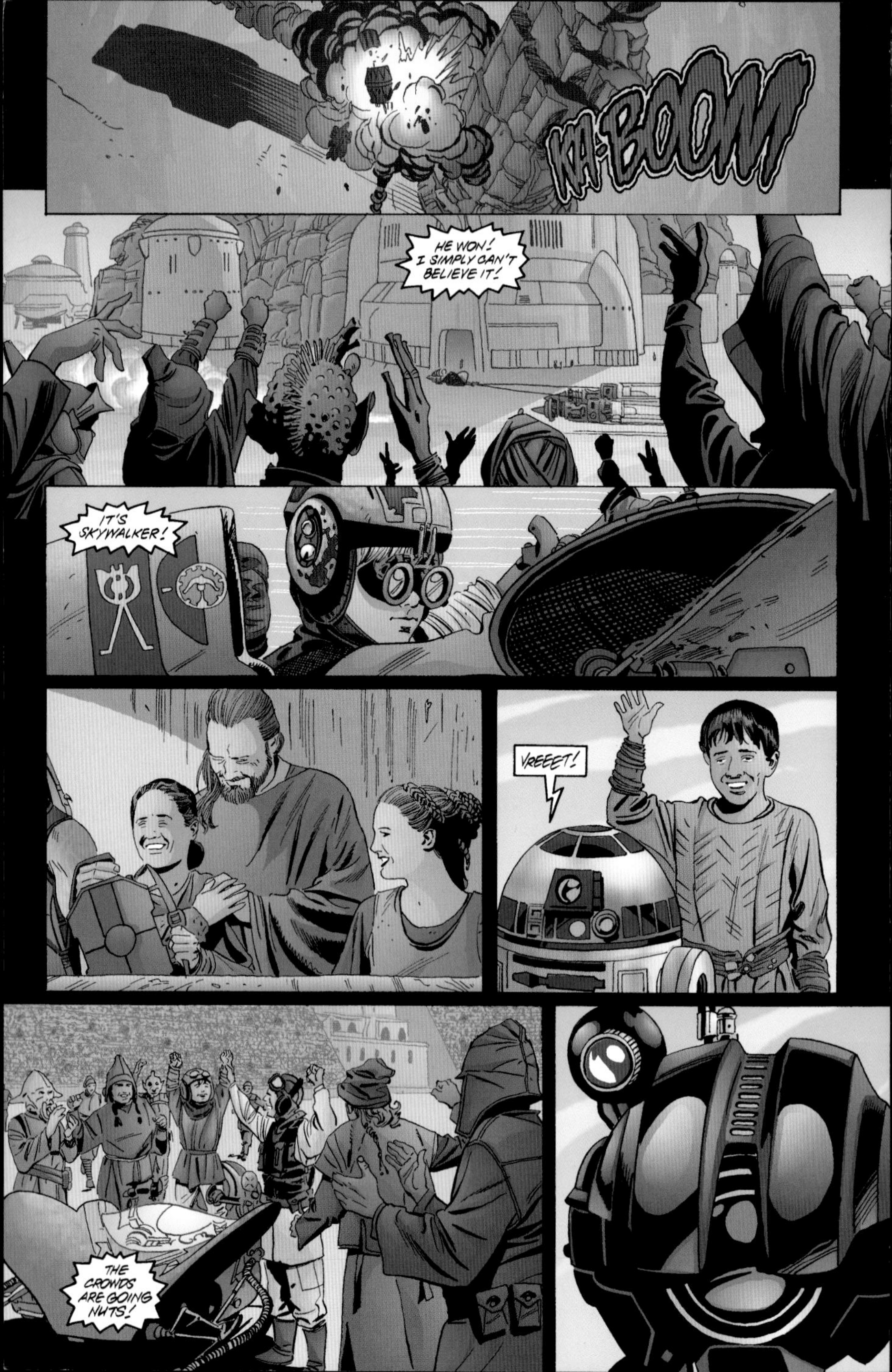
KA-BOOM
HE WON! I SIMPLY CAN'T BELIEVE IT!
IT'S SKYWALKER!
VREEET!
THE CROWDS ARE GOING NUTS!

THE CELEBRATION OF ANAKIN'S VICTORY CONTINUES...

WE OWE YOU EVERYTHING, ANNIE.

IT'S SO WONDERFUL, ANNIE. YOU HAVE BROUGHT HOPE TO THOSE WHO HAVE NONE. I'M SO VERY PROUD OF YOU.

NO KISSES!

OH, ANNIE...

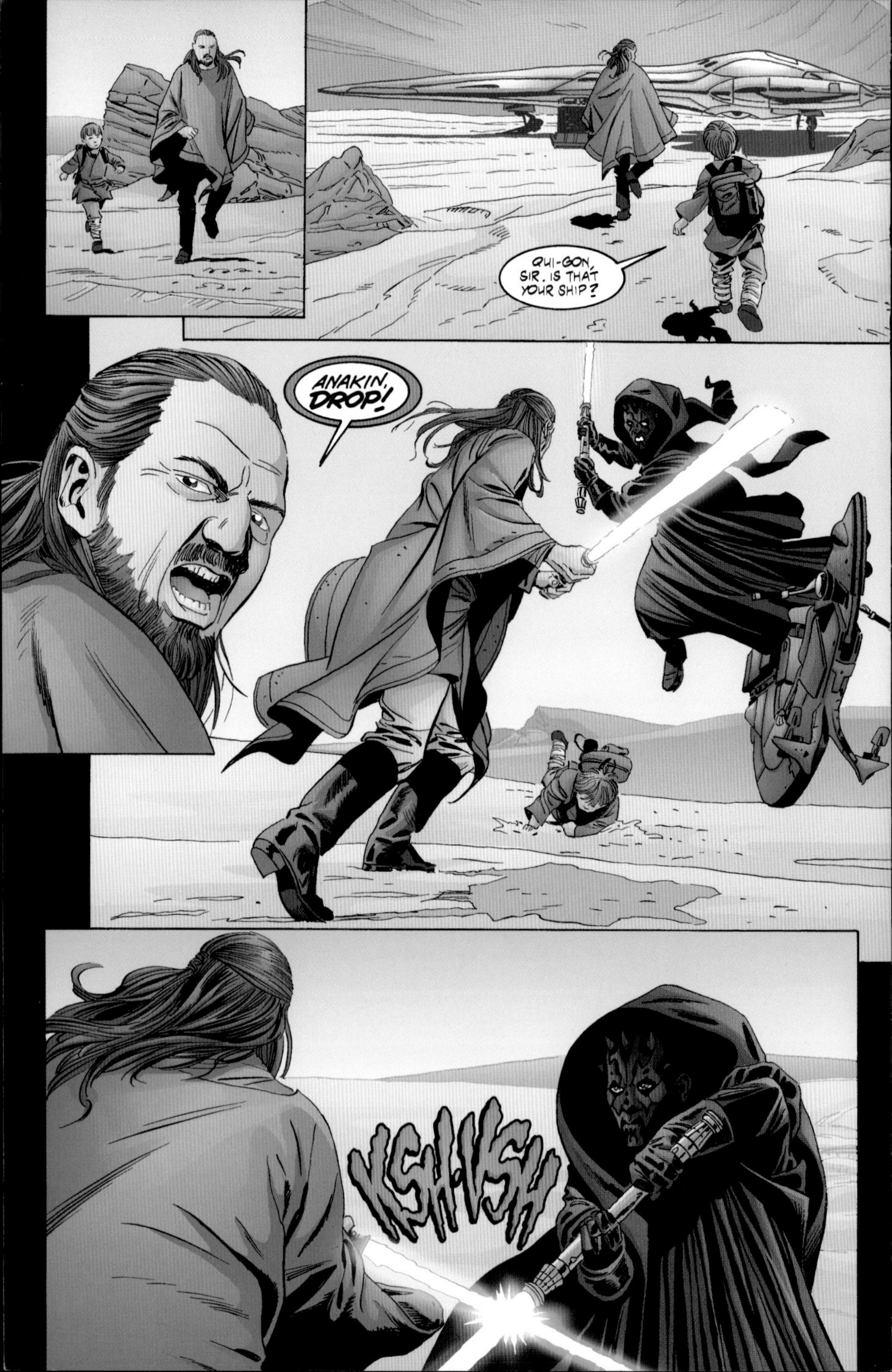

QUI-GON, SIR, IS THAT YOUR SHIP?
ANAKIN, DROP!
VSH-VSH

KSST

THUMP

BACK ON NABOO...

WHEN ARE YOU GOING TO GIVE UP THIS POINTLESS STRIKE? YOUR QUEEN IS LOST, YOUR PEOPLE ARE STARVING, AND YOU, GOVERNOR, ARE GOING TO DIE MUCH SOONER THAN YOUR PEOPLE, I'M AFRAID.

THIS INVASION WILL GAIN YOU NOTHING. WE'RE A DEMOCRACY. THE PEOPLE HAVE DECIDED.

MY TROOPS ARE IN POSITION TO BEGIN SEARCHING THE SWAMPS FOR THESE RUMORED UNDERWATER VILLAGES... THEY WILL NOT STAY HIDDEN FOR LONG.

TAKE HIM AWAY!

WHILE ABOARD THE QUEEN'S SHIP, HEADED FOR CORUSCANT...

THEY'VE CUT OFF ALL FOOD SUPPLIES UNTIL YOU RETURN. YOU MUST CONTACT ME.

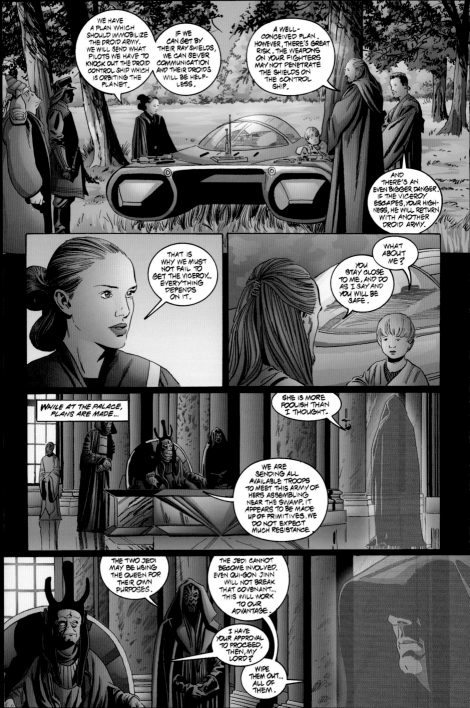

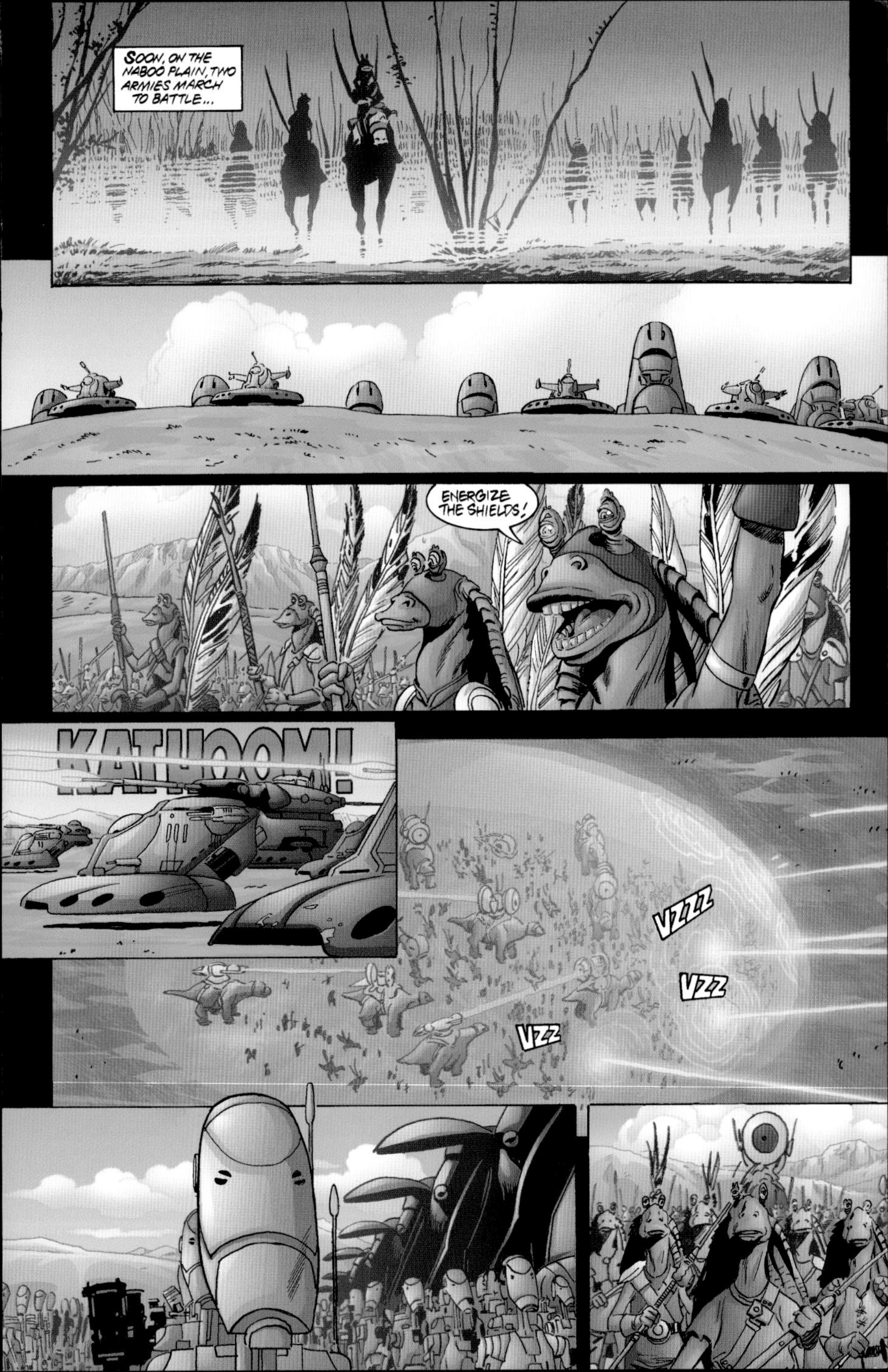

SOON, ON THE NABOO PLAIN, TWO ARMIES MARCH TO BATTLE...
ENERGIZE THE SHIELDS!
KATHOOM!
VZZZZ
VZZ
VZZ

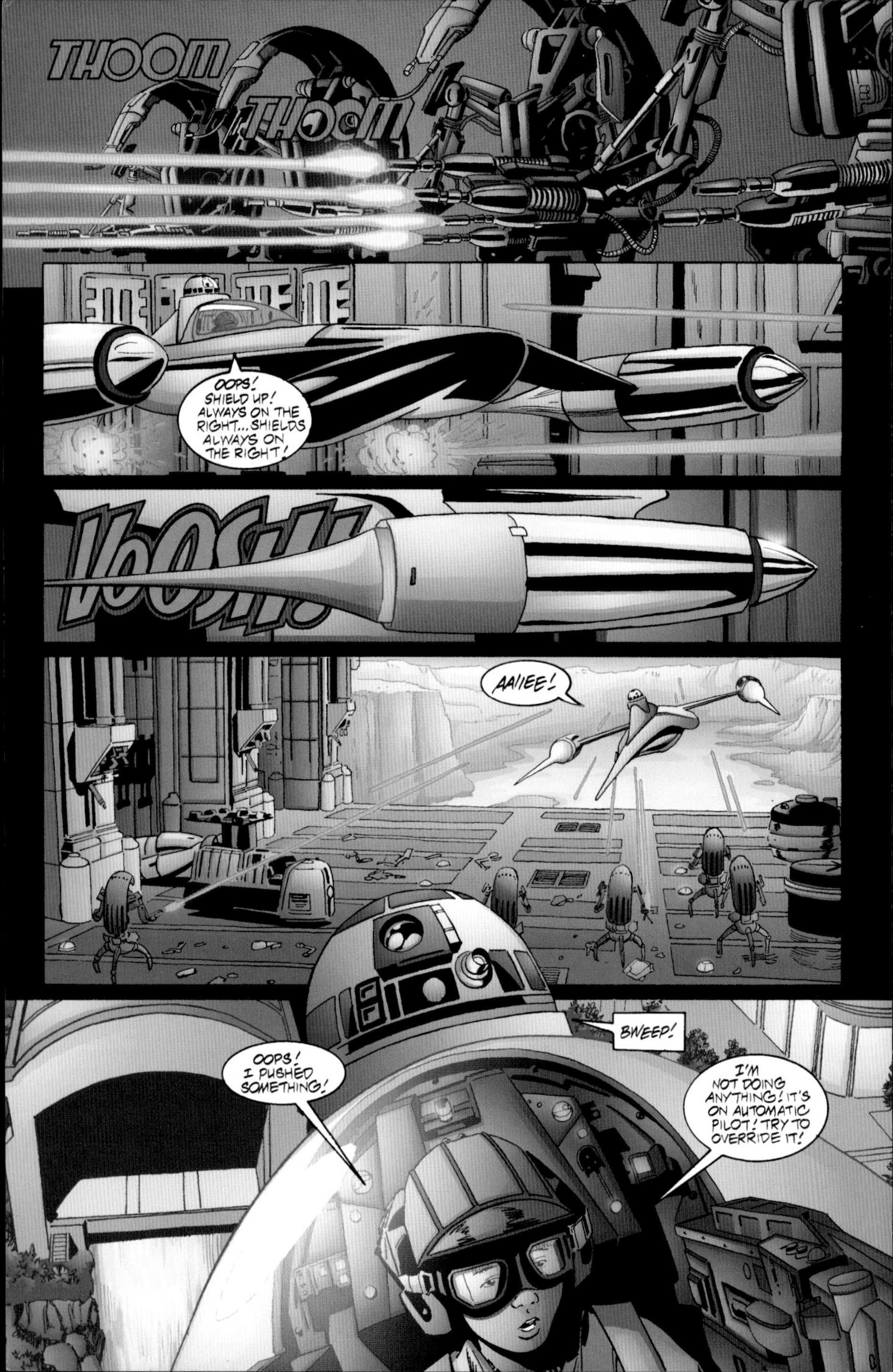
THOOM
THOOM
OOPS! SHIELD UP! ALWAYS ON THE RIGHT... SHIELDS ALWAYS ON THE RIGHT!
VOOSH
AAIIEE!
BWEEP!
OOPS! I PUSHED SOMETHING!
I'M NOT DOING ANYTHING! IT'S ON AUTOMATIC PILOT! TRY TO OVERRIDE IT!

VIPT

BAM

VPPT

WHILE AT THE PALACE...

WE DON'T HAVE TIME FOR THIS, CAPTAIN.

ABOVE NABOO...

YES, I'VE GOT CONTROL. YOU DID IT, ARTOO!

VREET-DOOP!

GO BACK?! QUI-GON TOLD ME TO STAY IN THIS COCKPIT AND THAT'S WHAT I'M GONNA DO. NOW C'MON!

WHOO, BOY! THIS IS TENSE! ARTOO, GET US OFF AUTO-PILOT!

BWEEP?

BACK ON THE NABOO PLAIN THE BATTLE RAGES.

OH, NO...

BMAM MAM

VVZ

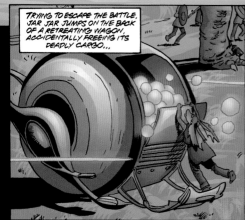

TRYING TO ESCAPE THE BATTLE, JAR JAR JUMPS ON THE BACK OF A RETREATING WAGON, ACCIDENTALLY FREEING ITS DEADLY CARGO...

OOOPS.

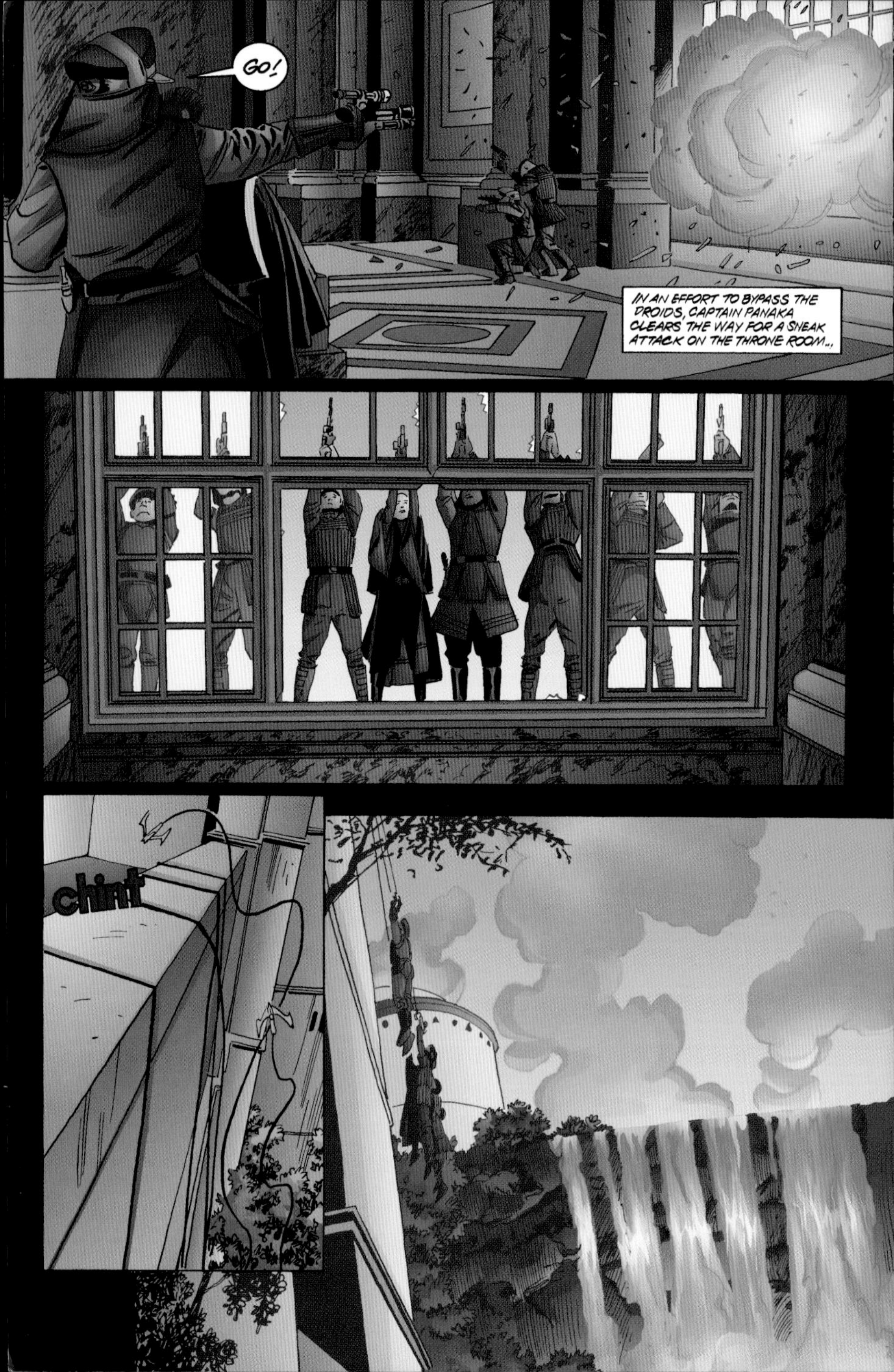
GO!
IN AN EFFORT TO BYPASS THE DROIDS, CAPTAIN PANAKA CLEARS THE WAY FOR A SNEAK ATTACK ON THE THRONE ROOM...
chint

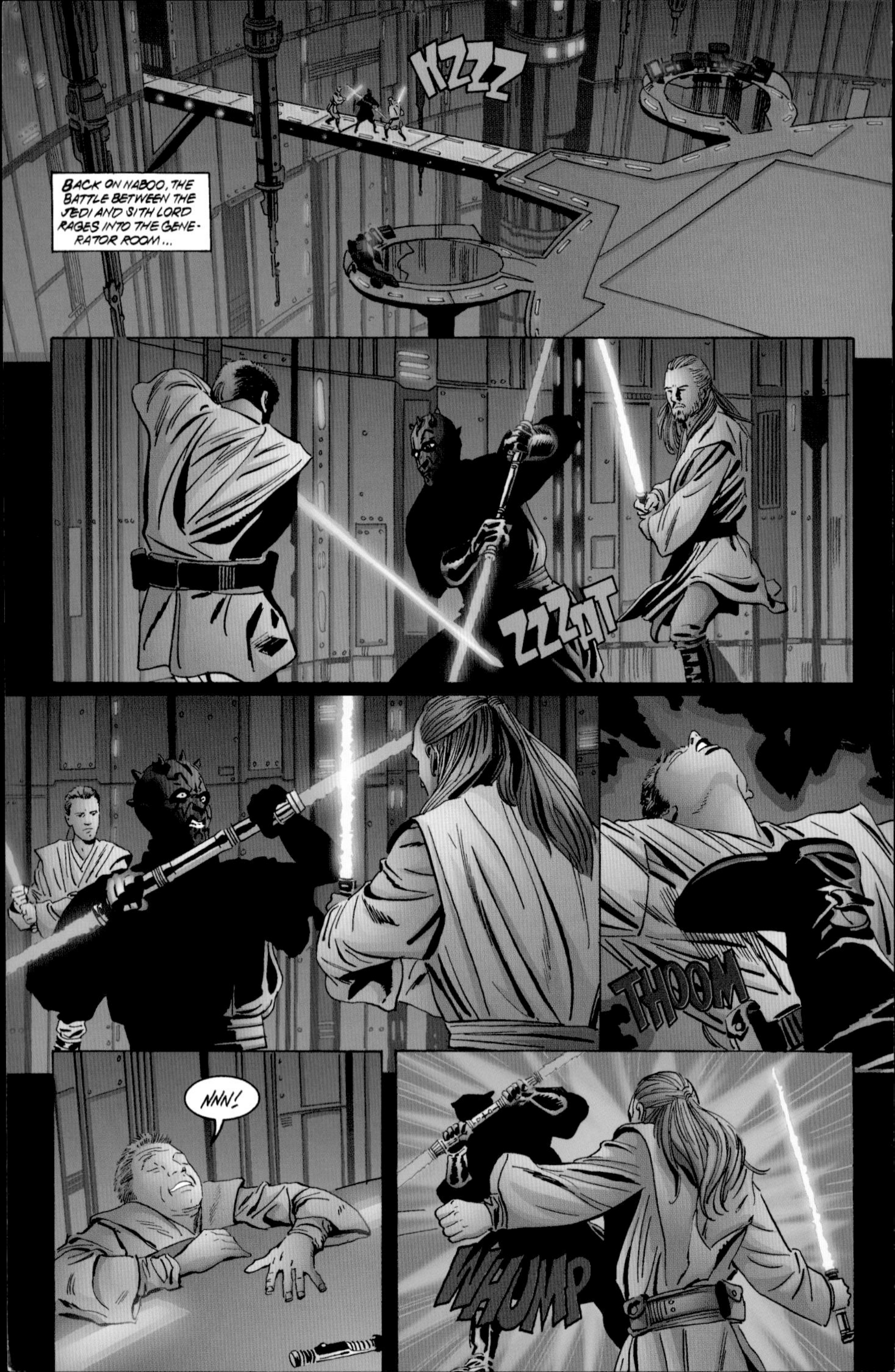
HZZZ
BACK ON NABOO, THE BATTLE BETWEEN THE JEDI AND SITH LORD RAGES INTO THE GENERATOR ROOM...
ZZZAT
THOOM
NNN!
WHUMP

VZZZ

QUI-GON FORCES THE
SITH LORD BACK, FURTHER
INTO THE GENERATOR
ROOM, DANGEROUSLY
NEAR THE DEADLY, PULSING
CONTAINMENT BEAMS...

BRIEFLY, THE BEAMS CUT THE
THREE COMBATANTS OFF FROM
ONE ANOTHER, OFFERING A
RARE PAUSE IN THE BATTLE.

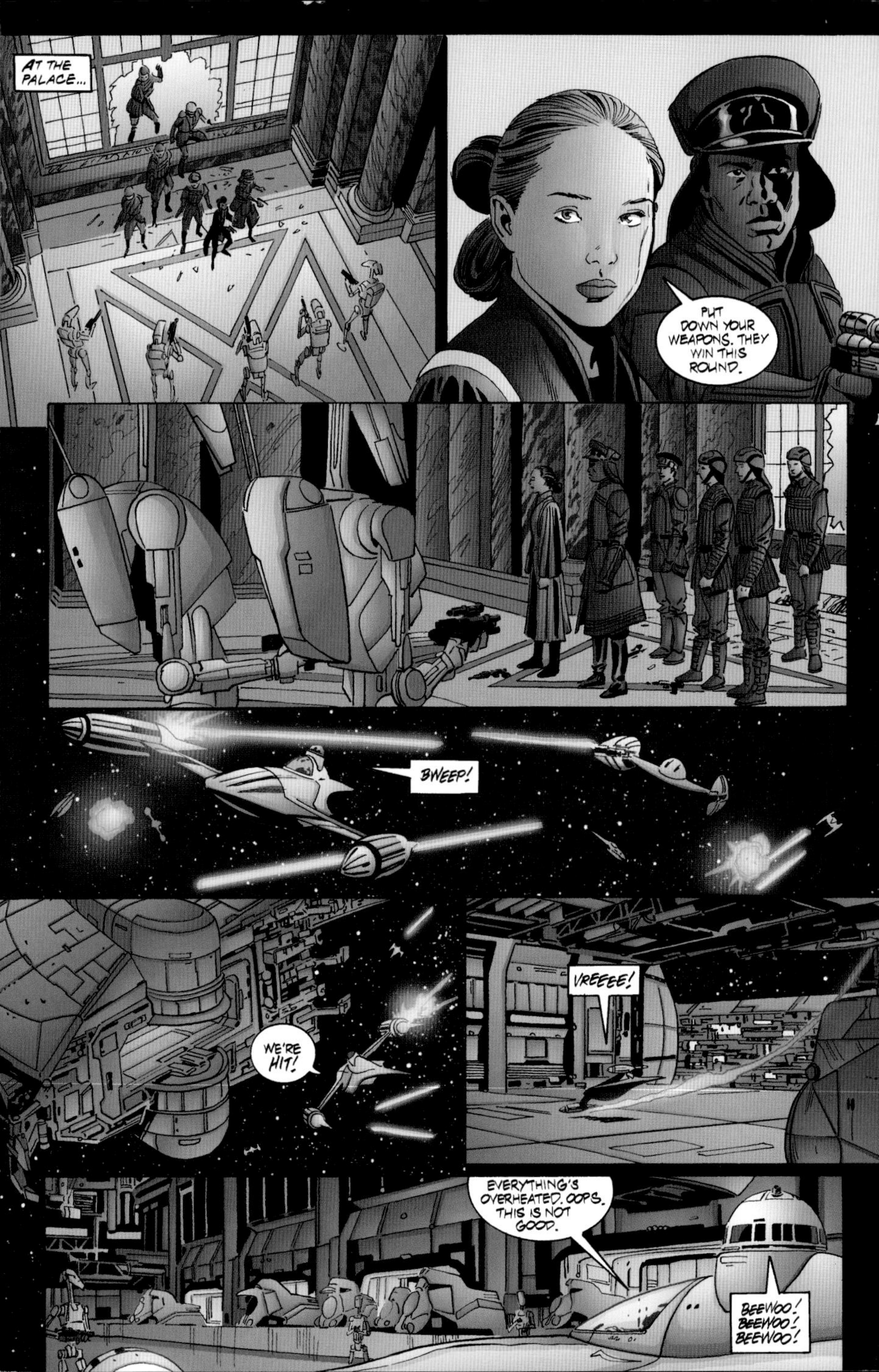
AT THE PALACE...
PUT DOWN YOUR WEAPONS. THEY WIN THIS ROUND.
BWEEP!
WE'RE HIT!
VREEEE!
EVERYTHING'S OVERHEATED. OOPS. THIS IS NOT GOOD.
BEEWOO! BEEWOO! BEEWOO!

VZZZZ

IN THE GENERATOR ROOM, THE CONTAINMENT BEAM FALLS FROM BETWEEN QUI-GON AND THE SITH LORD, AND THEIR BATTLE RESUMES...

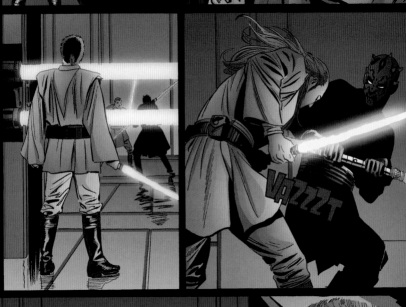

VAZZZT

NO!

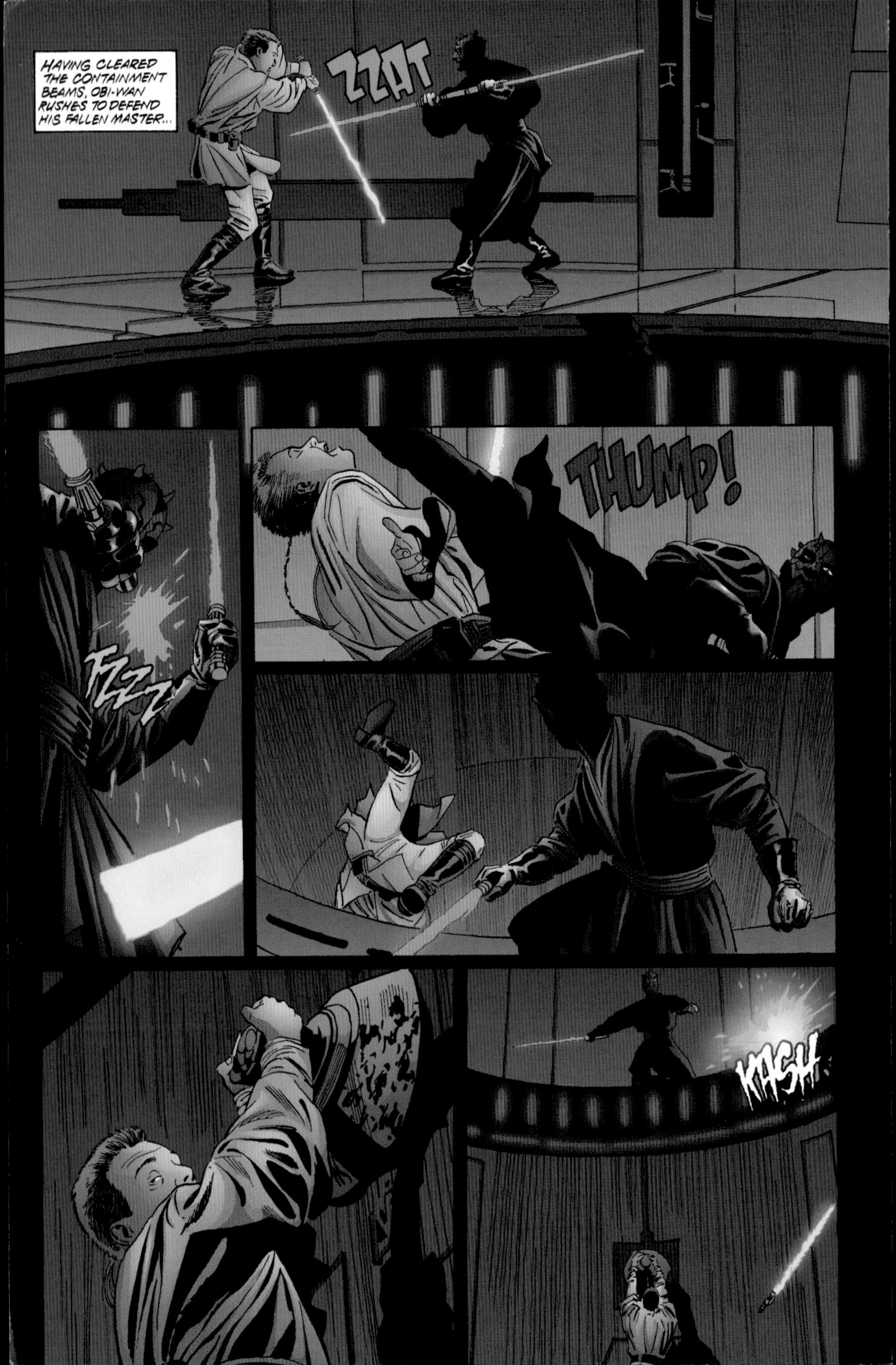
HAVING CLEARED THE CONTAINMENT BEAMS, OBI-WAN RUSHES TO DEFEND HIS FALLEN MASTER...
ZZAT
THUMP!
FZZZ
KASH

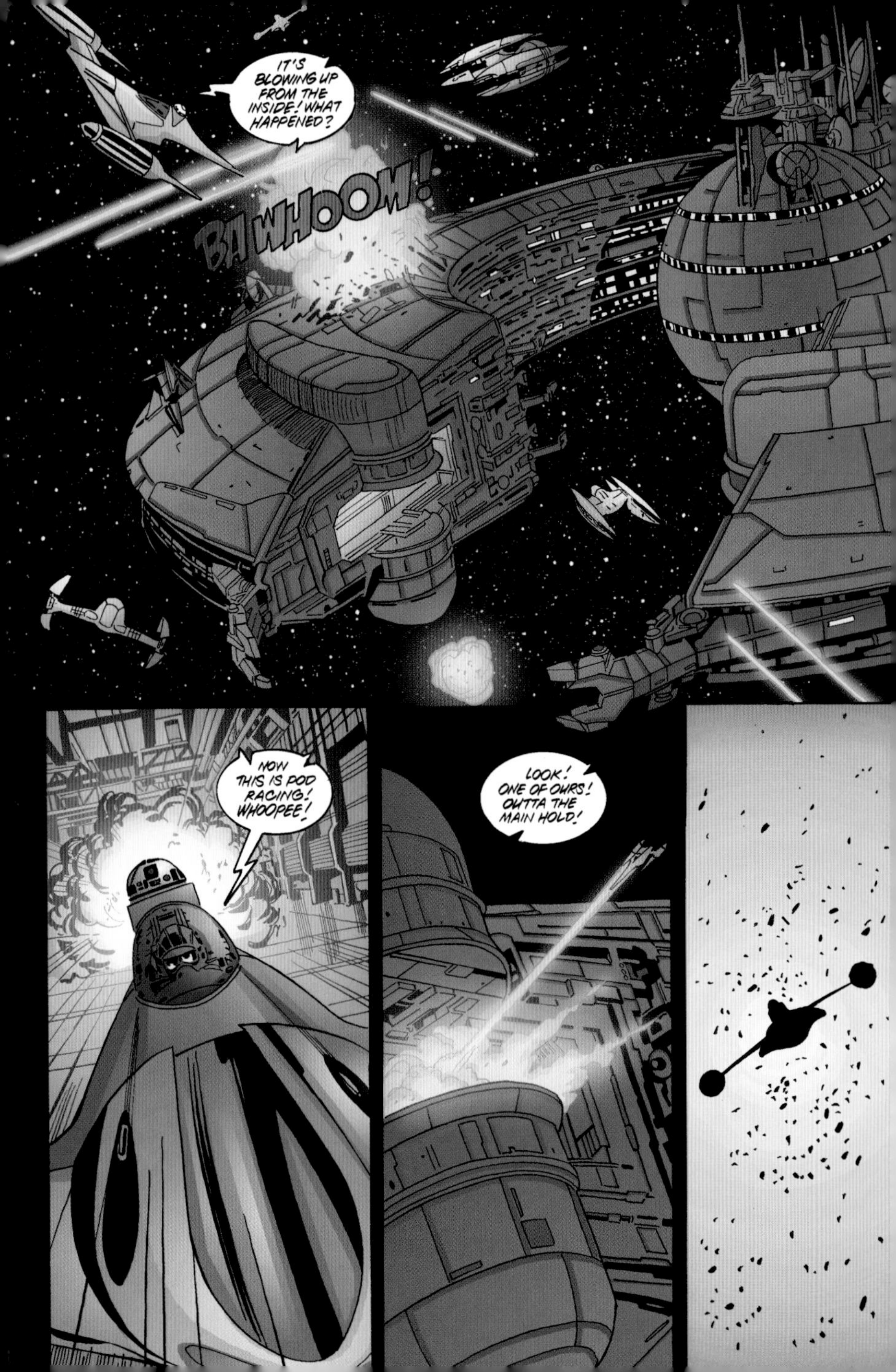
IT'S BLOWING UP FROM THE INSIDE! WHAT HAPPENED?
BA WHOOM!
NOW THIS IS POD RACING! WHOOPEE!
LOOK! ONE OF OURS! OUTTA THE MAIN HOLD!

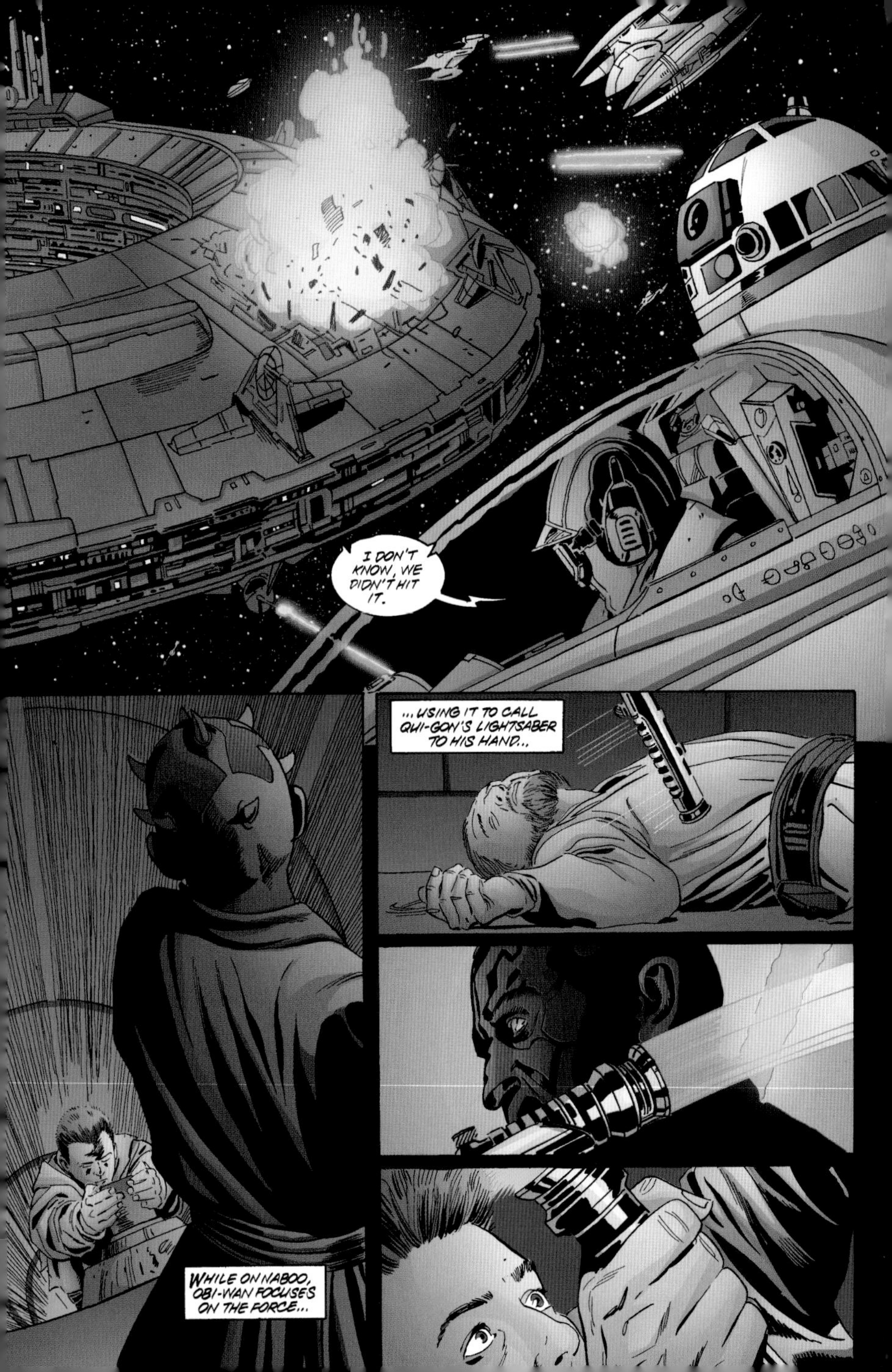
I DON'T KNOW, WE DIDN'T HIT IT.
WHILE ON NABOO, OBI-WAN FOCUSES ON THE FORCE...
...USING IT TO CALL QUI-GON'S LIGHTSABER TO HIS HAND...

FFZZZT

...AND, WITH THE AID OF THE FORCE, OBI-WAN LEAPS FROM THE PIT AND HALVES THE SITH LORD IN ONE SWIFT MOVEMENT...

MASTER! MASTER!

IT'S TOO LATE... IT'S...

NO!

OBI-WAN... PROMISE... PROMISE ME YOU'LL TRAIN THE BOY.

...YES, MASTER.

HE IS THE CHOSEN ONE... HE WILL... BRING BALANCE... TRAIN HIM...

WITH THE DESTRUCTION OF THEIR CONTROL SHIP, THE DROIDS ON THE NABOO PLAIN BEGIN TO MALFUNCTION...

BUT MESA DO A NUTIN'.

LATER, NEAR THE PALACE...

VICEROY, YOU ARE GOING BACK TO THE SENATE AND EXPLAIN ALL OF THIS.

I THINK YOU CAN KISS YOUR TRADE FRANCHISE GOODBYE.

CONGRATULATIONS ON YOUR ELECTION, CHANCELLOR.

YOUR BOLDNESS HAS SAVED OUR PEOPLE, YOUR MAJESTY. IT IS YOU WHO SHOULD BE CONGRATULATED. TOGETHER WE SHALL BRING PEACE AND PROSPERITY TO THE REPUBLIC.

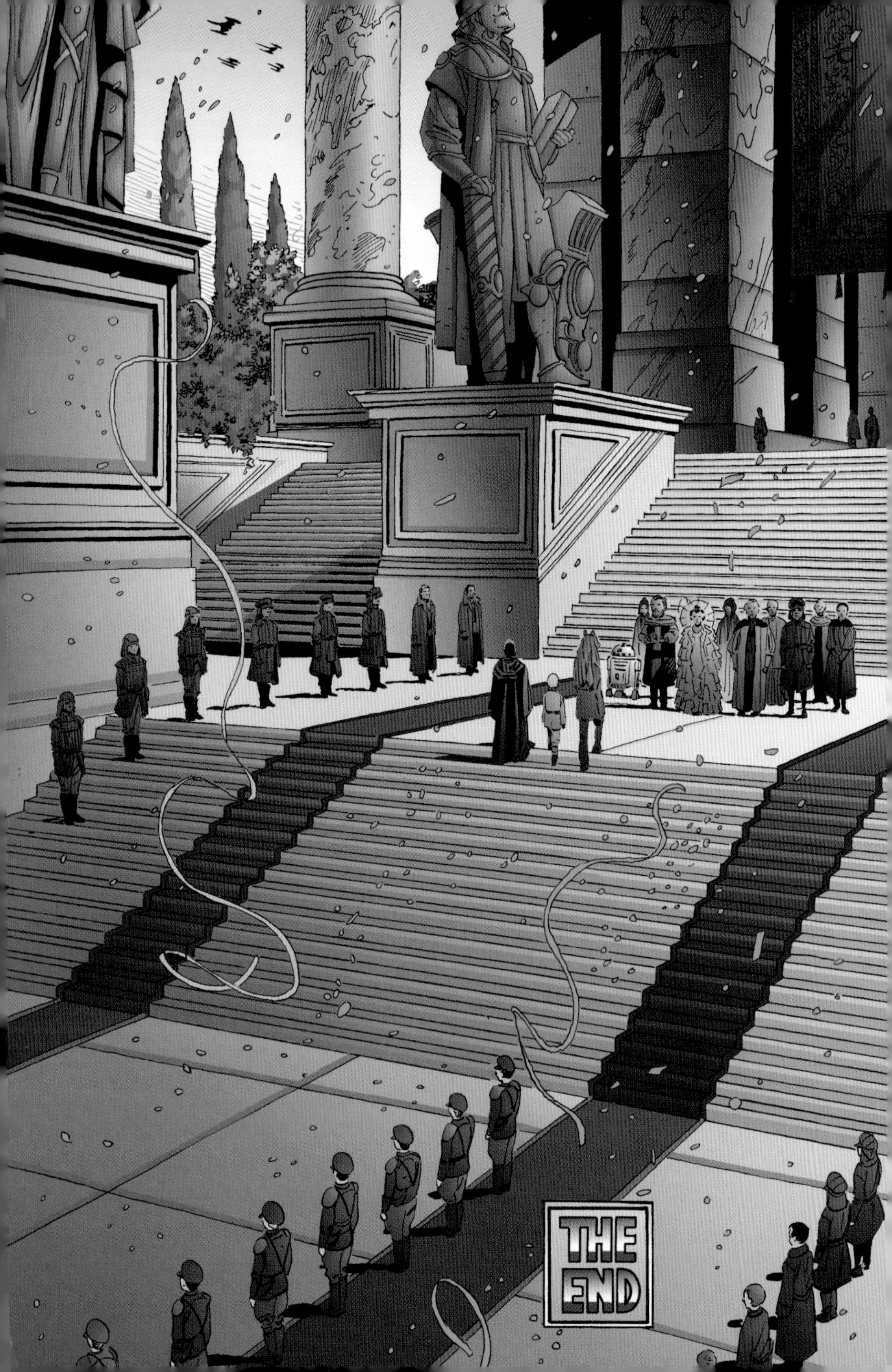
THE END

STAR WARS GRAPHIC NOVEL TIMELINE (IN YEARS)

Omnibus: Tales of the Jedi—5,000–3,986 BSW4

Knights of the Old Republic—3,964–3,963 BSW4

The Old Republic—3653, 3678 BSW4

Knight Errant—1,032 BSW4

Jedi vs. Sith—1,000 BSW4

Omnibus: Rise of the Sith—33 BSW4

Episode I: The Phantom Menace—32 BSW4

Omnibus: Emissaries and Assassins—32 BSW4

Omnibus: Quinlan Vos—Jedi in Darkness—31–30 BSW4

Omnibus: Menace Revealed—31–22 BSW4

Honor and Duty—22 BSW4

Blood Ties—22 BSW4

Episode II: Attack of the Clones—22 BSW4

Clone Wars—22–19 BSW4

Clone Wars Adventures—22–19 BSW4

General Grievous—22–19 BSW4

Episode III: Revenge of the Sith—19 BSW4

Dark Times—19 BSW4

Omnibus: Droids—5.5 BSW4

Omnibus: Boba Fett—3 BSW4–10 ASW4

Underworld—1 BSW4

Episode IV: A New Hope—SW4

Classic Star Wars—0–3 ASW4

Omnibus: A Long Time Ago . . . —0–4 ASW4

Empire—0 ASW4

Rebellion—0 ASW4

Omnibus: Early Victories—0–3 ASW4

Jabba the Hutt: The Art of the Deal—1 ASW4

Episode V: The Empire Strikes Back—3 ASW4

Omnibus: Shadows of the Empire—3.5–4.5 ASW4

Episode VI: Return of the Jedi—4 ASW4

Omnibus: X-Wing Rogue Squadron—4–5 ASW4

Heir to the Empire—9 ASW4

Dark Force Rising—9 ASW4

The Last Command—9 ASW4

Dark Empire—10 ASW4

Crimson Empire—11 ASW4

Jedi Academy: Leviathan—12 ASW4

Union—19 ASW4

Chewbacca—25 ASW4

Invasion—25 ASW4

Legacy—130–137 ASW4

Old Republic Era
25,000 – 1000 years before
Star Wars: A New Hope

Rise of the Empire Era
1000 – 0 years before
Star Wars: A New Hope

Rebellion Era
0 – 5 years after
Star Wars: A New Hope

New Republic Era
5 – 25 years after
Star Wars: A New Hope

New Jedi Order Era
25+ years after
Star Wars: A New Hope

Legacy Era
130+ years after
Star Wars: A New Hope

Vector
Crosses four eras in the timeline

Volume 1 contains:
Knights of the Old Republic Volume 5
Dark Times Volume 3

Volume 2 contains:
Rebellion Volume 4
Legacy Volume 6

BSW4 = before *Episode IV: A New Hope*. ASW4 = after *Episode IV: A New Hope*.

FOR MORE ADVENTURE IN A GALAXY FAR, FAR, AWAY . . .

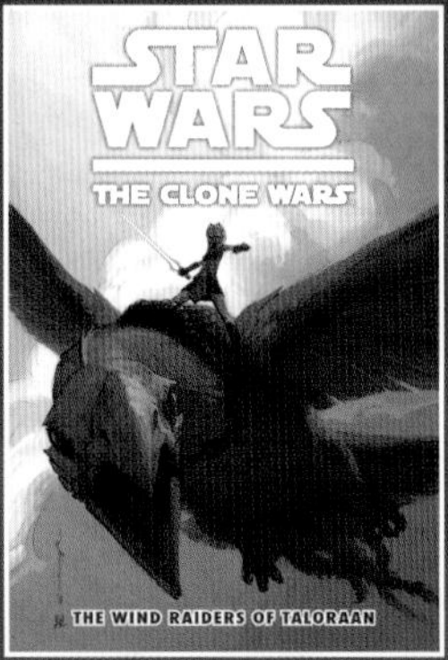
STAR WARS
THE CLONE WARS
THE WIND RAIDERS OF TALORAAN

STAR WARS: THE CLONE WARS—THE WIND RAIDERS OF TALORAAN
978-1-59582-231-4 | $7.99

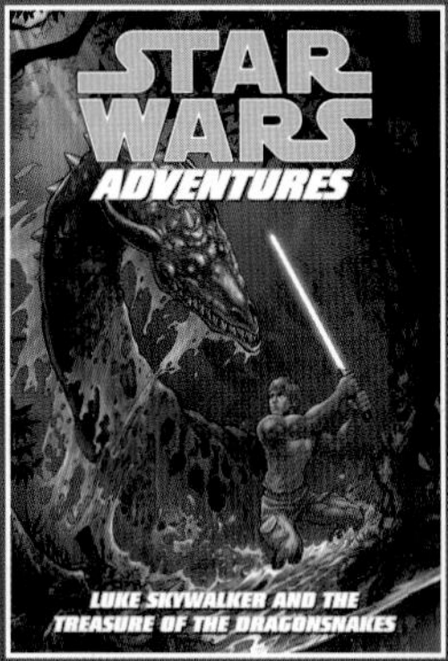
STAR WARS
ADVENTURES
LUKE SKYWALKER AND THE TREASURE OF THE DRAGONSNAKES

STAR WARS ADVENTURES: LUKE SKYWALKER AND THE TREASURE OF THE DRAGONSNAKES
978-1-59582-347-2 | $7.99

STAR WARS ADVENTURES: HAN SOLO AND THE HOLLOW MOON OF KHORYA
978-1-59582-198-0 | $7.99

STAR WARS ADVENTURES: PRINCESS LEIA AND THE ROYAL RANSOM
978-1-59582-147-8 | $7.99

STAR WARS ADVENTURES: THE WILL OF DARTH VADER
978-1-59582-435-6 | $7.99

STAR WARS: THE CLONE WARS—THE COLOSSUS OF DESTINY
978-1-59582-416-5 | $7.99

STAR WARS: THE CLONE WARS—SHIPYARDS OF DOOM
978-1-59582-207-9 | $7.99

STAR WARS: THE CLONE WARS—CRASH COURSE
978-1-59582-230-7 | $7.99

STAR WARS: THE CLONE WARS—SLAVES OF THE REPUBLIC
978-1-59582-349-6 | $9.99

STAR WARS: THE CLONE WARS—IN SERVICE OF THE REPUBLIC
978-1-59582-487-5 | $7.99

STAR WARS: THE CLONE WARS—HERO OF THE CONFEDERACY
978-1-59582-552-0 | $7.99

STAR WARS: THE CLONE WARS—DEADLY HANDS OF SHON-JU
978-1-59582-545-2 | $7.99

DARK HORSE BOOKS
darkhorse.com

AVAILABLE AT YOUR LOCAL COMICS SHOP OR BOOKSTORE

To find a comics shop in your area, call 1-888-266-4226
For more information or to order direct: • On the web: darkhorse.com • E-mail: mailorder@darkhorse.com
Phone: 1-800-862-0052 Mon.–Fri. 9 AM to 5 PM Pacific Time.

STAR WARS®

CLONE WARS ADVENTURES

Don't miss any of the action-packed adventures of your favorite STAR WARS® characters, available at comics shops and bookstores in a galaxy near you!

STAR WARS
CLONE WARS
ADVENTURES
Vol 4
STAR WARS
CLONE WARS
ADVENTURES
Vol 1
THREE NEW STORIES! ALL-JEDI ACTION!
STAR WARS
CLONE WARS
ADVENTURES
Vol 10
CLONES, DROIDS, AND BOUNTY HUNTERS
IN FOUR FANTASTIC TALES!

$6.99 each!

Volume	ISBN
Volume 1	ISBN 978-1-59307-243-8
Volume 2	ISBN 978-1-59307-271-1
Volume 3	ISBN 978-1-59307-307-7
Volume 4	ISBN 978-1-59307-402-9
Volume 5	ISBN 978-1-59307-483-8
Volume 6	ISBN 978-1-59307-567-5
Volume 7	ISBN 978-1-59307-678-8
Volume 8	ISBN 978-1-59307-680-1
Volume 9	ISBN 978-1-59307-832-4
Volume 10	ISBN 978-1-59307-878-2

AVAILABLE AT YOUR LOCAL COMICS SHOP OR BOOKSTORE
To find a comics shop in your area, call 1-888-266-4226
For more information or to order direct: • On the web: darkhorse.com • Phone: 1-800-862-0052 Mon.–Fri. 9 AM to 5 PM Pacific Time.
• E-mail: mailorder@darkhorse.com *Prices and availability subject to change without notice.

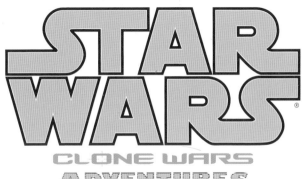

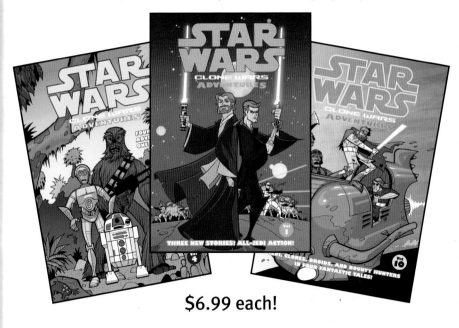